DATE DUE

This book belongs to:

....

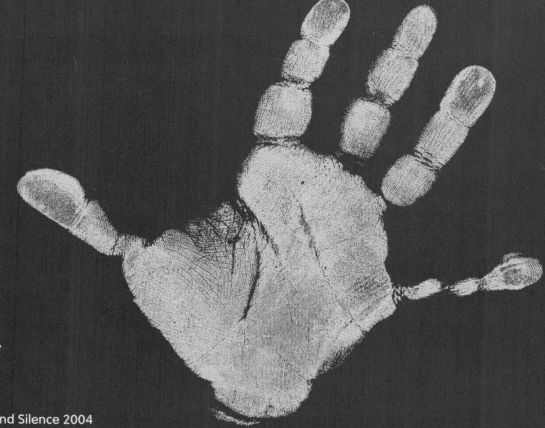

First published 2004 by order of the Tate Trustees
by Tate Publishing, a division of Tate Enterprises Ltd,
Millbank, London SW1P 4RG
www.tate.org.uk/publishing

British Library Cataloguing in Publication Data
A catalogue record for this book is available from the British Library

ISBN 1 85437 556 3

Distributed in the United States and Canada by Harry N. Abrams inc., New York

Library of Congress Cataloging in Publication Data
Library of Congress number applied for

Photography by Ella Doran
www.elladoran.co.uk
Design and Illustration by Silence
www.silence.co.uk
Printed by Imago

IS
FOR
ARTIST
an alphabet

Photography Ella Doran Design & Illustration Silence

artist

balloons

book

blocks   butterflies

C

colouring

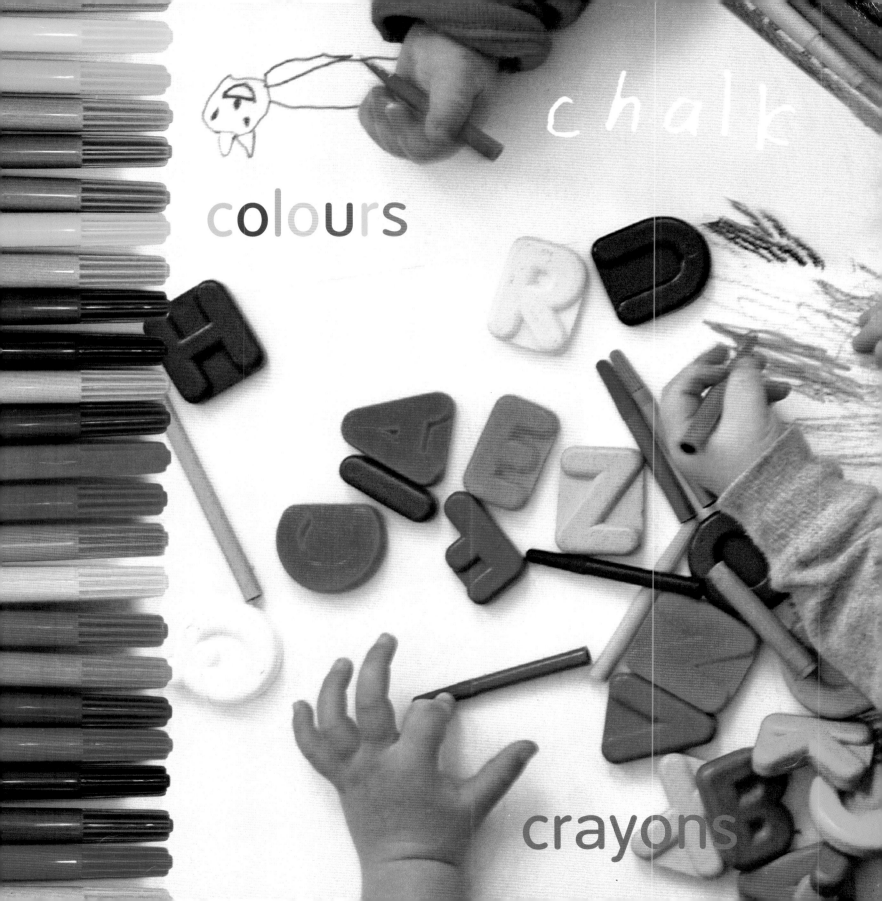

colours

chalk

crayons

dolls

exhibition

F

felt
field
flowers

grass grows **G**

H

house

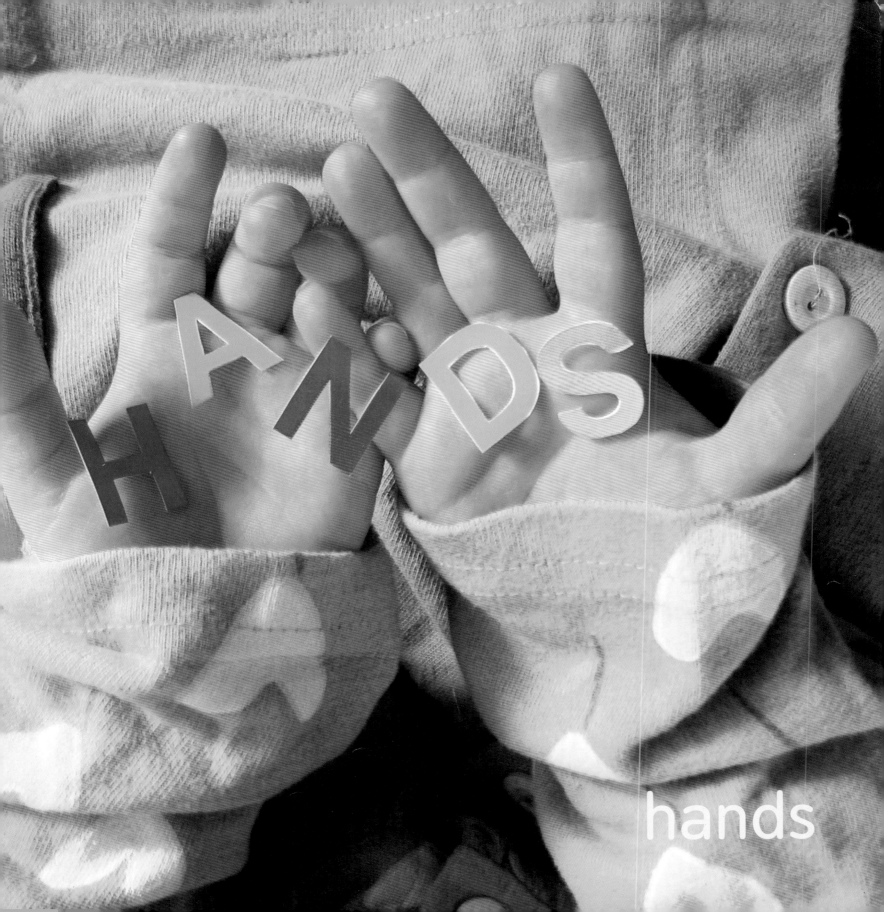

hands

What can you imagine? Draw with chalk on this page, then wipe clean with a dry cloth.

imagine

jungle

K kite

lollipop❤

M

marbles milkmaid **mouse** me

MASTER MOUSE

M E

moustache mask **money box** mushroom monkey

3

numbers

nest

OWL OWL OWL
OWL OWL OWL
OWL OWL
OWL OWL OWL

O

twitt-twoo twitt-twoo twitt-twoo
twitt-twoo twitt-twoo twitt-twoo
twitt-twoo twitt-twoo twitt-twoo
twitt-twoo twitt-twoo
twitt-twoo twitt-twoo
twitt-twoo twitt-twoo
twitt-twoo

owl

patchwork
paperclips
pins
paper
printing

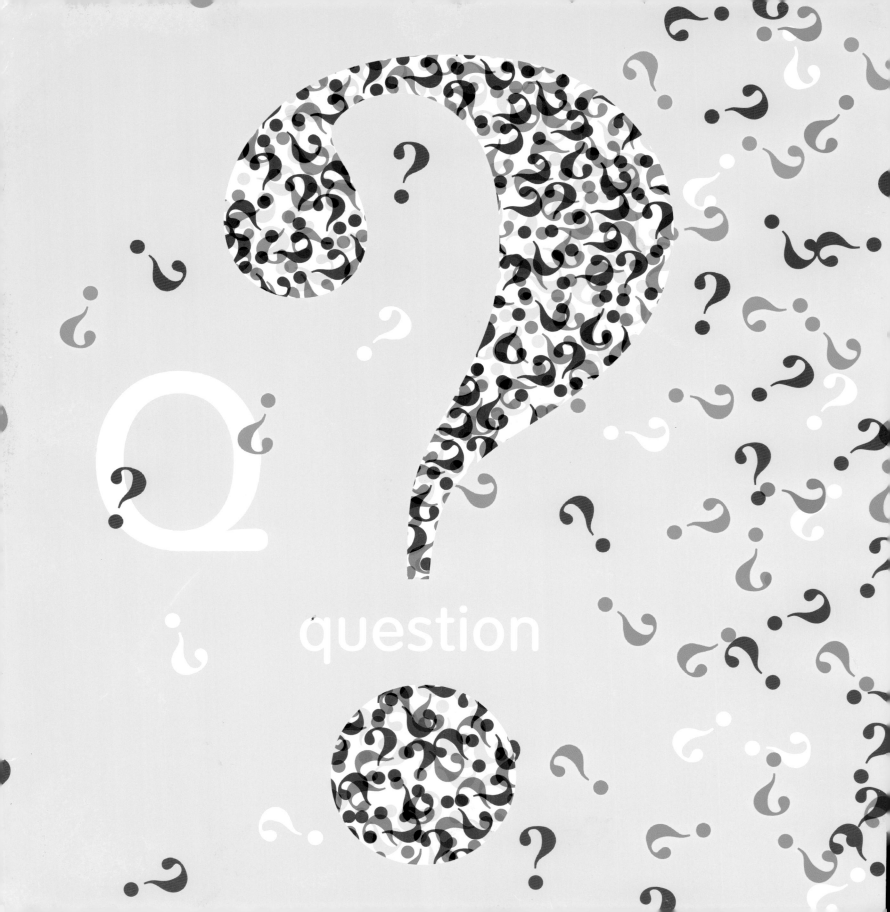

question

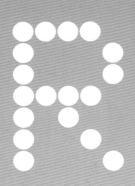

robot

recycle

rai bow

REDREDREDREDREDREDREDREDREDREDREREDREDREDREDREDREDREDREDREDREDREDREDREDRED
ORANGEORANGEORANGEORANGEORANGEORANGEORANGEORANGEOR
YELLOWYELLOWYELLOWYELLOWYELLOWYELLOW
GREENGREENGREENGREENGREENGREEN
BLUEBLUEBLUEBLUEBLUEBLUEBLUEBLUE
INDIGOINDIGOINDIGOINDIGOINDIGOIND
VIOLETVIOLETVIOLETVIOLETVIOLETVIO

ROAD

shoes
spots
stitch
stripes

string

shadow

T

train

teddy

turtle

U

umbrella

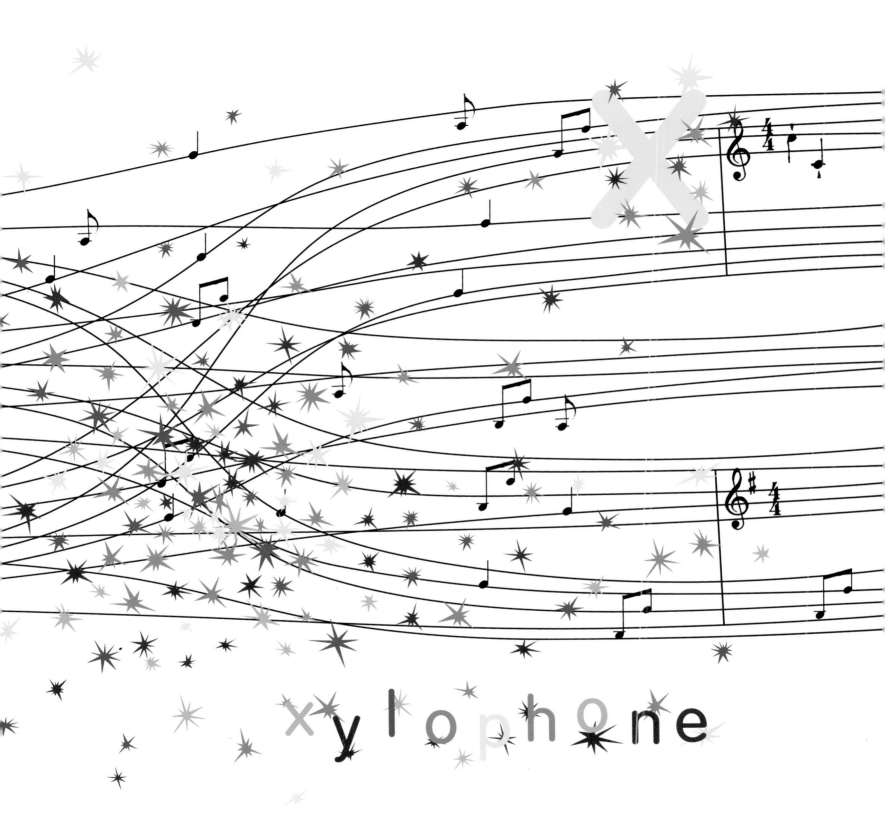

xylophone

yoyo

P

P

zip

zebra

ZEBRA

ZEBRA

A BIG THANK YOU

To: Olive Alvarez-Inwards, Camillia BenBassat, Annie Botta, Maya Borbon,
Joan and Derek Doran, Rob Doran, Tashi Doran, Michael Gibson, Robin Goldberg,
Jan and Howard Goodman, Hannah Goodman, Michelle Goodman,
Joelle Green, Mara Green, Happy Days Nursery, Ben Hawks, Vega Hertel,
Dan Holliday, Delilah Holliday, Mat Holliday, Melodie Holliday, Sam Holliday,
Saul Holliday, Simon Holliday, Ursula Holliday, Zoe Hope, Jeff Kazimir, Joseph Khan,
Daniel Kwagan, Jacob Martin, Andy McLeod, Olivia McLeod, Rachel McLeod,
Stan McLeod, Eve and Brian Miller, Saul Miller, Lenny Mitchell, Barney Quinton,
Kitty Quinton, Jada Smith, Nel Stewart, Anna Wadsworth.

ABCDEFGHIJKLMNOPQ
RSTUVWXYZABCDEF
GHIJKLMNOPQRSTU
VWXYZABCDEFGHIJK
LMNOPQRSTUVWXYZA
BCDEFGHIJKLMNOPQR
STUVWXYZABCDEFG
HIJKLMNOPQRSTUVWX
YZABCDEFGHIJKLMNOPU